Inventions That Changed the World

Pearson Education Limited
Edinburgh Gate, Harlow,
Essex CM20 2JE, England
and Associated Companies throughout the world.

ISBN 0 582 85489 X

First published by Penguin Books 2005

Text copyright © David Maule 2005

Typeset by Ferdinand Pageworks, Surrey, UK
Set in 11/14pt Bembo
Printed in Spain by Mateu Cromo, S. A. Pinto (Madrid)

Produced for the Publishers by
Clare Gray Publishing Services Ltd, London, UK

Published by Pearson Education Limited in association with
Penguin Books Ltd, both companies being subsidiaries of Pearson Plc

Acknowledgements
Every effort has been made to trace the copyright holders and we
apologise in advance for any unintentional omissions. We would be
pleased to insert the appropriate acknowledgement in any subsequent
edition of this publication.
We are grateful to the following for permission to
reproduce photographs:
Getty Images: page 2 (Hulton Archive);
Science Museum/Science and Society Picture Library:
pages 21, 25, 27, 40, 49 (Bletchley Park Trust), 56;
TRH Pictures: page 34.

For a complete list of the titles available in the Penguin Readers series please write to your local
Pearson Education office or to: Penguin Readers Marketing Department, Pearson Education,
Edinburgh Gate, Harlow, Essex, CM20 2JE.

Contents

Introduction

Bayliss had a new idea for a radio. You turned a handle a number of times and this produced enough electricity to make it work.

Today you can walk into an electrical equipment store and buy a radio which has no wires or batteries. These radios seem so simple that you might wonder why nobody thought of them before. But it took the inventor Trevor Bayliss a long time to turn his idea into a working model. It was even more difficult to make a company believe in it. Now many people in poorer countries, who live in areas without electricity and who can't afford batteries, can listen to the news and get advice on health, business, or farming. The new radio has changed their world.

Inventors are unusual people. They look at things that we all see, and they think of something new. Then they often have to work for years to turn their ideas into something that works. They might spend all their money and still not find a company that believes in their new product. Sometimes inventors start their own companies to sell their ideas. They can make a lot of money doing this—or lose everything they have.

People invent for all kinds of reasons. Some want to discover more about the world around them. Others want to communicate more easily. Some want to make life better for all of us. Others are simply looking for power and money.

Whatever the reason is, many inventors have ideas that change our lives. This change is not always an improvement; inventions can be used to harm people as well as to help them. Some inventions, though, have really changed the world. This book is about them.

Chapter 1   Printing

When personal computers first appeared, people began to talk of
the "paperless office." Everything would be done on computer,
and there would be no need for paper copies. This didn't happen.
The new computers came with desktop printers and now more,
not fewer, pages are printed. The story of printing is a long one,
and it continues today.

The beginning

Imagine that you are a printer working in China around a
thousand years ago. Paper, a Chinese invention, has already been in
use for hundreds of years. You produce printed books, but these
are very expensive because they are difficult to make. To print just
a single page of a book, you have to take a wooden board and cut
into it until all the words and pictures stand up from the wood.
After that, you spread ink over the board, turn it upside down onto
a piece of paper, and press hard. And when you have made boards
for all the other pages, and printed enough copies of the book,
there is no possibility of reusing them. This system is quicker than
writing each book by hand, but it is still very slow. It takes you and
the other printers a very long time to make one book.

Fortunately, sometime between the years 1041 and 1048, a
man called Bi Sheng had an idea. He started to make small
blocks, and on each of these he cut one word. To form a page, Bi
Sheng put a number of smaller blocks together. After the page
was printed, the blocks could be used again.

The new method quickly spread through China, then into
Korea, Vietnam, the Philippines, and Japan. With reusable type,
books and education became much cheaper, so many ordinary
people were able to get better jobs.

Gutenberg

By the fifteenth century, block printing had appeared in Europe, where it was used to make playing cards and a small number of books. Johannes Gutenberg was the first person to work with reusable type. Maybe he had heard of the Chinese invention, but it is also possible that he had the same idea himself.

Gutenberg's father was in charge of making coins in Mainz, Germany, so the son knew about metal from an early age, and he

Gutenberg's printing press

was later trained to make gold jewelry. As a result, he decided to use metal to make his reusable type. Recent progress in science had supplied new knowledge of different metals, but Gutenberg had to try many of these before he found the best.

He also used earlier inventions. His printing press was similar to the heavy presses that were used for making wine. Good-quality paper had recently appeared in Germany. This was made from old cloth. Before then, books had been printed on sheets of material made from animal skin, which took between three and four weeks to produce. Only the new paper could be produced quickly enough for the speed of Gutenberg's press.

In 1454, Gutenberg began to print a new Bible. It is known as the "42-line Bible" because of the number of lines on a page. He made around 180 copies. Of these, 48 still exist, either complete or in parts. All of them are slightly different. Some were printed on animal skin, but most are on paper. Also, the large capital letters and some other details were added by hand, and different artists had different ideas. These Bibles are now the most valuable printed books in the world. In 1987, one incomplete copy sold for $5,390,000 in New York.

Gutenberg himself made nothing out of his great invention. He had borrowed money to start his business from a lawyer called Johann Fust. When he was unable to repay this on time, he had to give Fust his press, his tools, and his materials. He died a poor and forgotten man in 1468. Fust continued Gutenberg's work and, in 1457, he was the first person to print in color, using red and blue ink as well as black.

Printing spreads

The invention of printing spread quickly through Western Europe, and by the year 1500 there were 1,000 print shops. These had already produced around 201 million copies of 35,000 different books. This had a great social effect. By 1530, 60% of the population of Europe was able to read.

The first English printer was William Caxton, who learned the job in Germany and opened a press in England in 1476. He printed almost 100 books, mainly on literature and religion. He translated some of these himself from French and Dutch.

In Venice, in 1494, Aldus Manutius started a business called the Aldine Press. Until then, books had been large and were kept indoors. Manutius began to produce smaller, cheaper books that could be carried around in people's pockets. At first, he printed new copies of the works of Plato, Aristotle, and other Greek and Latin writers. He later produced informative books on subjects like shipbuilding. When these appeared, people wrote to him with corrections and suggestions, which were printed in later copies of the book. This meant that information began to move around at a much faster speed. The Aldine Press has been described as an early kind of Internet.

In 1638, a Mrs. Glover arrived in the United States. She had sailed from England with five children, a printer, some other workers, and a printing press. She had had a husband too, but he had died on the way across the Atlantic. Mrs. Glover's plans didn't end with his death, though, and she started America's first printing press at the new college of Harvard.

The nineteenth century and later

After Gutenberg, there were very few real improvements to printing until the nineteenth century. It had always been possible to include pictures by using cut wooden boards, which were later made of metal. In 1719, Jakob Christof Le Blon of Frankfurt, Germany, started using three separate blocks covered with blue, yellow, and red ink. These were pressed onto the paper one after another to produce fully-colored pictures.

The first water-powered press was suggested around 1500 by the Italian Leonardo da Vinci, and in time this was actually used. The next step forward didn't happen until 1810, when Frederick Koenig of Germany invented the steam press. The paper was placed around a tube, which then moved across the type. Soon afterward, Koenig began to use a second tube, so the press made a print forward and backward. John Walter, the owner of *The Times* newspaper in London, bought two steam presses in 1814. Each printed 1,100 sheets an hour.

At this time, printers couldn't work very quickly because all the pieces of type from one page had to be taken out and then put together again for the next page. In 1838, this changed when a new machine was invented in New York. This could heat the old type until it became liquid, and make new letters. It was much faster than the old system. Four years later, another machine was invented which could put the letters together. It had a keyboard like a piano and the operator only had to hit the keys to produce a page. For some time a second operator was needed to make the lines of type the same length. Then, in 1886, a new machine appeared which could do both operations at the same time. It could place 6,000 letters an hour and was soon in use around the world.

The enormous growth of printing led to a great increase in the amount of paper used for newspapers, magazines, and books. After 1970, so many trees were cut down that there was a danger of changing the world's climate. In recent years, people have worked hard to solve this problem.

At the end of the twentieth century there was a move away from "hot metal" to computerized printing, and the old methods began to pass into history. A printer used to be someone who could make readable pages out of hot metal. Now it is a desk-top machine that delivers good quality pages at high speed. The work of Gutenberg and his followers is now done inside a computer.

Chapter 2   Mathematics

Without mathematics, it may be possible to build a very simple house, road, or bridge, but greater understanding is needed for more complicated jobs. People realized this at a very early stage of human history, and their simple knowledge of numbers grew into the skills which allow us to build computers and use the Internet.

Pythagoras

In 525 B.C.,* the King of Persia led his army into Egypt and took many prisoners. One of them was a Greek mathematician, Pythagoras. Pythagoras was sent to Babylon, in modern-day Iraq, and there he had the opportunity to study two things which the Babylonians really knew about: mathematics and music. It is possible that he learned about right-angled triangles from the Babylonians. Some Babylonian writing, from at least a thousand years before his visit, says:

> 4 is the height and 5 is the longest side. How wide is it?
> Its size is not known.
> 4 times 4 is 16.
> 5 times 5 is 25.
> 16 from 25 leaves 9.
> 9 is 3 times 3.
> So 3 is the width.

But they never formally proved this.

In mathematics, the most common system of counting uses the number 10. We count up to 9, then we use the 1 again and start changing the second number—10, 11, 12 ... From the Sumerians, who had lived in the area before 3500 B.C., the Babylonians had taken a system which used 60.

They didn't have to learn sixty different signs. Each of their

* B.C.: years before the birth of Christ

numbers was built up from just two, one for "10" and one for "1." So when you reached 59, you had to write five "10" signs and nine "1" signs in a special arrangement, but the Babylonians didn't seem worried by this. The system was good enough to tell them about amounts of building materials, the number of workers necessary for a job, and how many days were needed to complete it.

After around five years, Pythagoras left Babylon and returned to his home on the Greek island of Samos. There he started a school of mathematics. But the Samians had a problem with his teaching methods, and they also wanted him to take part in local politics, so after two years he moved to Crotone, on the southern coast of Italy.

He started another school there, which took both male and female students. Some of them lived in the school all the time. They owned nothing and ate only vegetables. They were taught by Pythagoras himself and believed in certain ideas. One of these was that, at its deepest level, nature follows mathematical rules.

The teachings of Pythagoras came from this school. He wrote nothing himself, because the school was very secretive. Modern mathematics is interested in making up and solving mathematical problems. Pythagoras's school was interested in how mathematics worked and what it meant to prove something. This was a great step forward from the Babylonians, and the new mathematicians thought of right-angled triangles as three connected squares. Together, the areas of the squares on each of the shorter sides are the same as the area of the square on the longer side. This could easily be proved by cutting up the two squares and putting them together to make the third.

The Pythagoreans were making good progress toward a mathematical description of the world when they were stopped by a simple problem. If you have a right-angled triangle with two sides each of a length of 1, then $1^2 + 1^2 = 2$, so the length of the third side is $\sqrt{2}$. But this can't be given as a whole number. You

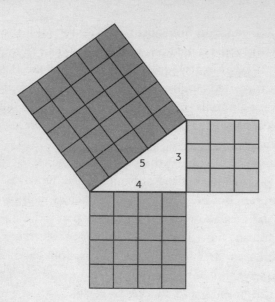

5 3
4

Proving the length of the third side of a right-angled triangle.

can start with √2 = 1.41421356237309504880168872420097 …
and you can continue forever. So you can only write this number
as √2. The Pythagoreans then discovered that √3, √5, √6, √7, and
√8 are also not whole numbers. So, some of the relationships in
nature couldn't be written down using numbers. This was a great
problem for their way of thinking.

Euclid

Around two hundred years after Pythagoras, a man called Euclid
lived in Alexandria, Egypt. Although his home was there, he was
Greek. He certainly traveled to Greece, and it is probable that he
spent some time studying with Plato in Athens. When he
returned to Alexandria, he started a school of mathematics and
wrote a great book on the subject, the *Elements*. This was still in

use in some schools in the twentieth century, and it has been said that after the Bible, it has been more studied, translated, and reprinted than any other book.

Many of the ideas in the *Elements* didn't start with Euclid. He wanted to bring all knowledge of mathematics together in a single book. He also introduced a new way of thinking, by proving an idea, then using this to help prove another one. This sounds simple enough to us today, but it was the beginning of the method of proving ideas that we still use.

The Romans

After the Babylonians, the Egyptians, and the Greeks, the Romans ruled the western world. They understood mathematics well enough, but they weren't very interested in it. Imagine a Roman engineer who has to build a wooden bridge across a small river. The Romans took their measurements from parts of the body—the length of a finger, a hand, a foot and, for longer distances, a double step. The bridge will be forty-four double steps long and four double steps wide. The pieces of wood to make the road are each two double steps long and one foot wide. There are five feet to each double step. So to reduce everything to Roman feet, you simply write

$$\frac{(44 \times 5) \times (4 \times 5)}{(2 \times 5)}$$

Unfortunately, you have to use Roman numbers, so it will actually look like this:

$$\frac{(XLIV \times V) \times (IV \times V)}{(II \times V)}$$

Of course, Romans didn't do it this way. Numbers were only used for writing down the answer. Instead, they used a simple machine or a counting board and within a few seconds got the answer of CDXL (440).

Roman engineers were highly skilled. They built roads, water systems, bath houses, and great buildings. But for them, as for the Babylonians, mathematics was a way of improving their buildings, not improving their minds. Pure mathematics, which began in Greece, wasn't reborn in Rome, but in the Middle East.

Al-Khwarizmi

For counting, we use nine numbers. Each of these numbers can have a different value according to its position—so the "1" in "100" isn't the same as the "1" in "10." This idea began in India around the year 500, and from there it moved to the Arab world. Around 786, a man called Al-Khwarizmi was born in Uzbekistan. Later he worked in a school in Baghdad, and there he wrote a book about using Indian numbers. When this book was translated into Latin, it introduced the idea into Europe.

Al-Khwarizmi is also known as "the father of algebra." In fact, the word *algebra* comes from *al-jabr*, part of the Arabic title of another book by Al-Khwarizmi. In this book, he describes two important ideas about equations. First, you can move things from one side to the other, which makes equations easier to solve: for example $4x^2 = 12x - 2x^2$ becomes $6x^2 = 12x$ (so $x = 2$). He also showed that you can make an equation easier by taking away the same amount from each side: for example, $x^2 + 4x + 40 = 11x + 30$ can be reduced to $x^2 + 10 = 7x$ (so $x = 5$).

Although Romans did little to add to our understanding of these new ideas, the ideas became more widely known when they were written in the Roman language, Latin. When the works of Pythagoras, Euclid, and Al-Khwarizmi appeared in Europe in Latin translation, they helped to move human progress forward.

Chapter 3   Navigation

Imagine that you are going to sail a boat across the ocean, and you can take with you either a watch or a compass. Which one do you choose? The answer, of course, is a watch. You can use it to find south, as any outdoor person knows. But it will tell you something else, something equally important. This knowledge has saved many sailors' lives.

The sun and the stars

If you can tell how high the sun is in the sky at noon, or the height of the North Star, Polaris, you know how far north or south you are. This fact was known to the earliest sailors. To measure this, Arabs used a piece of wood tied to the end of some string. By the sixteenth century, European sailors were using a similar tool, but made of two pieces of wood, with numbers marked along the longer one.

A thousand years before this, John Philoponos of Alexandria had described a new instrument which could take better measurements. It was in the form of a circle and had a map of the stars on it. This was also an Arab invention. You could use it to find the time of day, the time the sun came up or went down, and the direction of different places. Because it could tell the direction of Mecca, it was popular in the Middle East.

Although this instrument worked very well, it was quite expensive, and in time a simpler form appeared. This was shaped like a quarter-circle. It had a piece of string hanging down. You pointed the top edge of the instrument at a star, then held the string in place and read the measurement. But even this was too expensive for most European sailors, and they continued to use the simple tool made of pieces of wood.

An important improvement on this was invented in about

1594 by the English captain John Davis. He sailed a number of times to the Arctic and gave his name to the area of water between Greenland and Canada. Because it was very difficult to look straight into the strong Arctic sun, he decided that the navigator should use the shadow of the sun instead.

The navigator looked at the line between the ocean and the sky through the holes A and B. He then moved holes A and C until the sun shone through hole B. Then he added up the measurements on the two curved pieces of wood. This new instrument became very popular. It gave better measurements and it meant that navigators didn't have to look straight into the sun every day and maybe go blind in one eye.

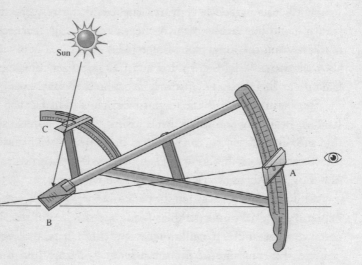

An instrument of navigation using the shadow of the sun

The compass and maps

Although all of these instruments worked more or less well, there isn't much difference in the Mediterranean between the height of the sun at noon in, for example, Genova in the north and Alexandria in the south. So early Mediterranean sailors also kept careful records of the movements of the ship. For this, they needed a map, a way of knowing their direction of travel, and a method for measuring the speed of the ship.

By the third century, Chinese scientists knew that a type of iron-rich stone had special qualities. They learned to cut a piece of this stone into the shape of a spoon with a very smooth bottom. This was placed on a smooth square metal plate. When the spoon turned and stopped, its handle pointed to the south. This was the first compass.

By the eleventh century, people realized that a very thin piece of metal could be placed on this stone, and in time it "learned" to do the same thing. If the piece of metal was then placed on water in a bowl, it also pointed north and south. Chinese ships commonly used compasses like these to tell which direction they were sailing in.

Some time later, the compass was known in Europe too. It seems that it was discovered independently on both continents, because the idea doesn't appear in Indian or Arab writings. By 1190, Italian sailors were using needles on bowls of water.

To tell a ship's speed, early sailors tied a piece of wood to some string with some knots in it, each one separated by the same distance. They then threw the wood over the side of the ship and counted the number of knots as the knots ran through their fingers. The number in a certain length of time told them the speed of the ship. This was done regularly, and the results were written in a book. Today, although instruments to measure speed have improved greatly, we still describe the speed of a ship in knots. A knot is equal to 1.85 kilometers an hour.

From a very early date, people knew that the world was round. In the third century B.C., the Greek scientist Eratosthenes decided that the distance around it was about 46,000 kilometers. This isn't very different from the correct figure of 40,000. Early map-makers, like Ptolemy in the first century, had to use their knowledge of the stars and travelers' reports of distance and direction to decide where places should appear. Naturally, they knew most about places which were closer to home. Europe, the Mediterranean area, and the Middle East were mapped quite well, but they thought the distance to the Far East was greater than it actually is.

All of this early knowledge was lost to the West when the Library of Alexandria was destroyed in a Roman war in the third century. For the next thousand years, western map-makers took many of their ideas from the Bible, filling their maps with places from it. In the Arab world, more scientific methods continued, and these were used for western map-making from the twelfth century, when Europeans began to read Arab writing.

Between 1271 and 1295, the Venetian Marco Polo traveled to the Pacific coast of China. He was able to give many details about distant countries, and these were added to the maps of the time.

The best maps were, of course, very expensive, and ordinary sailors used much simpler ones. These contained a lot of useful information about winds, the movement of the ocean, and the shape of the land when coasts were seen from a ship. It is interesting that the Chinese had similar guides at the time.

By the fifteenth century, quite good maps of large areas of the world were being produced, but there were still some problems. Christopher Columbus (Colón), a navigator from Genova, looked at the maps of the time and decided that he could reach Asia by traveling west. He was correct, but the position of the Far East was still uncertain. The maps told Columbus that it was 10,000 kilometers closer than it was. This is why, when he reached America, he thought that he had arrived in India.

Maps are, of course, flat, but the world is round. The Greeks and Romans had tried to solve this problem, but their maps weren't very good for navigation. In 1569, a Flemish map-maker called Gerard Mercator invented a new and very simple method, and his name can still be found on many maps of the world. He imagined putting a sheet of paper around the world, and then shining a light from the center of the earth through it. The different parts of the world could then be drawn on the paper.

A map like this has its faults. Countries nearer the North and South Poles* appear bigger than they really are. But a straight line on the map is also a straight line for traveling, which is a great advantage. So sailors could simply draw a line and then read the direction they wanted to go in. As well as for navigation, the Mercator map is still the most popular in the home and in school. It is how most of us see the world today.

East and west

For sailors, there was still the problem of how far east or west they were. They could only tell this by drawing the direction and speed of the ship on a map. But, over time, mistakes grew bigger and bigger, and quite often ships sailed straight into the land that they were trying to reach.

An example of this happened in 1707, when five British warships were returning from the Mediterranean. They had sailed for twelve days in fog. They hadn't seen the sun, the stars, or land in all that time, and they were very unsure of their position. The navigators on each ship had records showing speed and direction, so they compared their ideas, but they were wrong. As the ships continued north, the first one hit the rocks around the Scilly Islands off the southwest of England. Before anything could be

* North Pole, South Pole: the furthest north and south points of the Earth

15

done, three of the others had followed. Two thousand men died.

This was only one of many terrible events. Sometimes ships crashed into rocks; in other cases they simply got lost, sailing until men died of hunger. But this time four warships had been destroyed close to home. Ships' owners and officers put more pressure on the British government, and in 1714 a new law was passed. This promised a prize of £20,000 (around $2.7 million today) to anyone who could find a solution.

The problem is actually quite a simple one. The world turns around once every twenty-four hours. Each place in the world is at a different time within those twenty-four hours. In any part of the world, you can tell when it is noon by looking at the sun. If you know that it is midnight in London, and the sun is above you, it means that you are near the middle of the Pacific. If it is 3 P.M. in London, you are in the middle of the Atlantic. So you only need a way of knowing the time in London. But that, for the sailors of the time, was an enormous problem.

There were two possible ways of solving it. One way was to use the stars. In 1610, Galileo discovered that Jupiter had four moons. He studied these for a year, noting when they disappeared behind Jupiter, and wrote down the times. He told his plan to King Philip of Spain, who was also offering a prize to the discoverer of a solution. Galileo's idea wasn't accepted because of the difficulty of seeing Jupiter's moons from ships, although it was used by map-makers on land. Later in the seventeenth century, special buildings were opened in Greenwich and Paris, where scientists could watch the stars with the aim of helping ships tell their position. The scientists made little progress. Their solutions meant checking the position of a number of stars—which wasn't easy on a moving ship and was impossible in bad weather—and then doing a lot of difficult mathematical work.

The other method was to make a clock or a watch that worked on the ocean. It had to be unaffected by changes in temperature, air pressure, or the movement of a ship. The problem was finally solved by an English clockmaker, John Harrison, who between 1737 and 1770 built a number of better and better clocks and watches. But the scientists didn't like Harrison. He was only a clockmaker. They argued against his solution to the problem, and as a result he was only given half of the prize. He only received another £8,750 when he was an old man, after the king spoke for him.

Although the first of these new watches were expensive, they were used more and more as time passed. When Captain James Cook sailed to the Pacific for the second time in 1772, he took a watch similar to one that Harrison had made. He found that the method worked very well.

Radar and satellites

Through the nineteenth century and into the twentieth century, ships and later airplanes continued to navigate by using the height of the sun for north and south and watches for east and west. Better instruments were produced for checking the sun, but little else changed. The next step forward wasn't taken until the Second World War (1939–1945), when radar was invented.

An airplane could either fly along a radar signal, or find its position from the strength of two signals which were sent out from different places. Since radar signals travel in straight lines, though, the curve of the earth limited its usefulness to a few hundred kilometers.

When satellites were sent up above the earth, this problem was solved. Today the world is covered by twenty-four of these satellites and their ground stations. Now, a hand-held receiver, costing less than $100, can measure the travel time of a signal from them and tell you your position to within a few meters anywhere on Earth. Navigation has come a long way from a piece of wood on the end of a piece of string.

Chapter 4 Guns

Sometimes, the most unlikely people think of terrible things. In 1805, John Forsyth invented a way of making guns fire better and in all weathers. He was a church minister. Richard Gatling, who built the first machine gun, was a doctor. Wars lead to rapid progress, but people suffer and die. Is this a fair price to pay? Whatever we think, the story of the gun is part of human history.

Gunpowder

Chinese scientists first discovered that when you lit certain materials, they produced a lot of gas very quickly. The Chinese also realized that if these materials were put into a container and lit, they could blow the container to pieces.

In a Chinese book from 1044, three ways of making gunpowder are discussed, although gunpowder probably existed for at least two hundred years before this. The first bombs were made by filling wooden tubes with gunpowder and pieces of iron. These were then shot from a bow. There were also true rockets, which were powered by gunpowder.

In 1126, a man called Li Gang wrote that he ordered the people of the city of Kaifeng to "fire cannon" at the Nuzhen people who were attacking them. Many of the Nuzhens died. Within the next hundred years, cannon were produced which were strong enough to make holes in the walls of a city.

The invention of gunpowder helped the Chinese to keep their northern neighbors, the Mongols, out of their country for many years. In time, though, the Mongols took Chinese gunpowder-makers prisoner, learned how to make gunpowder themselves, and then used it against the Chinese. As the Mongols moved west, gunpowder traveled with them.

Guns in Europe

The method of making gunpowder arrived in the Arab world in the twelfth century. In England Roger Bacon, who is sometimes called the first English scientist, read about it in Arabic writing and so brought the idea west.

The first cannon appeared in Europe soon after this—copies of the guns used by the Arabs. These were made in the same way as a wooden barrel, with a number of long pieces of metal held together by round pieces. This is why, even today, we use the word *barrel* for the long part of a gun.

This method of making them meant that the cannon had a number of weak points and might blow up easily. To try to stop this happening, they were very heavy. Since they were expensive to make, needed a team of skilled men, and could only move around very slowly, they were more useful for attacking cities than enemy armies. From their first appearance, castles began to be less useful in protecting cities.

Cannon were placed on European ships almost as soon as they appeared, and their use increased, sometimes with terrible results for the ship. Special openings were cut into the sides of ships so they could fire out. In 1545, King Henry VIII's finest warship, the *Mary Rose*, sank because she was carrying too many guns.

There were many similar problems, but guns continued to be used in greater and greater numbers. In 1805, Nelson's ship, the *Victory*, fought at Trafalgar with 104 guns. Gunfire rarely sank wooden ships, though. Most ships were simply hit and hit again until they couldn't move and most of the sailors were dead.

Handguns

The first handguns, which appeared in the fourteenth century, were simply smaller cannon. The metal barrel was held under the arm and a match was put to a hole at the back. Not surprisingly, there was little chance of hitting anything. Then a wooden piece was fitted to the back so that the gun could be fired from the shoulder. Later, the match was fixed to a moveable metal part. This made it easier to touch it down on the gunpowder. This type of gun, known as a "matchlock," had a much greater chance of hitting the enemy.

When guns first appeared, the most powerful killing machine in Western Europe was the Welsh longbow, and later the English longbow. This could hit a man at least 300 meters away and pass through metal plate at distances of over fifty meters. A good bowman could do this fifteen times a minute, and the result was usually death in large numbers. But to pull a bow as powerful as this, a man had to practice day after day from about the age of fourteen. The bodies of long-dead bowmen have recently been dug up, and they show that the bow changed the shape of the men's backbones.

Although the matchlock was much slower, a man could be taught to use it in a very short time. The chances of hitting anybody were smaller, but its killing power was much greater. Although it was possible to make metal plate thick enough to stop a bullet, it was uncomfortably heavy. During the sixteenth century, guns became more popular than bows.

The problem with the matchlock was that the match had to be lit first, and taken care of all the time. Inventors looked for ways to solve this. The result, early in the sixteenth century, was the "wheel-lock." In this new gun, a rough metal wheel was turned against a material which produced fire—in exactly the same way as a cigarette lighter works. This meant that the gun could be carried ready to fire.

The wheel-lock, though, was expensive to produce, and it didn't work every time. The next important invention appeared in the late sixteenth century. In this, a piece of stone struck against

A "flintlock" gun, in which stone struck metal

a metal plate. This type of gun was much simpler and cheaper to make. If it wasn't raining, it usually worked, and guns like this were used for the next two and a half centuries.

By the 1820s, a new firing method had appeared. Small pieces of metal were filled with gunpowder, which caused an explosion when they were struck. These weren't affected by the weather, and they were much simpler, so it was now easier to produce guns which fired many times. In 1836 Samuel Colt, of Connecticut, US, invented a simple type of handgun which fired five or six bullets one after another. By the middle of the century, guns of this type were commonly used and became part of the story of the American West. We are all familiar with movies where the hero uses a gun made by Colt. There is even a saying in the US: "Abraham Lincoln made men free. Sam Colt made them equal."

The rifle

In the early nineteenth century, bullets were round. Because they had to be pushed in from the open end of the gun, they didn't fit tightly. This space around the bullet meant that it didn't fly very straight when it was fired. Back in the sixteenth century, a new gun had appeared which had curved lines cut into the inside of the barrel. These made a quarter turn as they went from end to end, so the bullet turned as it left the gun. This meant that a bullet could fly much straighter and kill at a greater distance. There was a disadvantage, though, because it was difficult to push the bullet down the barrel. It took much longer to prepare this new gun—called a rifle—for firing, so rifles were mainly used for hunting.

Many years later, though, this began to change. During the War of Independence of 1775–83, Americans used their hunting rifles against British soldiers and found they could hit their enemies from a long distance. The British learned from the experience, and riflemen fought in Portugal, Spain, and France from 1807 to 1814. Dressed in green uniforms, they were taught to move out ahead of the army and work independently.

Next, a gun was needed where the bullet didn't have to be pushed down the barrel. It was easy enough to make a gun that could be opened, but there was an escape of gas from loose gunpowder and the bullet didn't travel as far. So the bullet and the gunpowder were put inside a metal tube. This produced a bullet as we know it today.

Although repeating rifles didn't work well enough for armies to use them until toward the end of the nineteenth century, even a single-shot rifle could now fire fairly quickly and kill at a long distance. So soldiers couldn't stand in straight lines and shoot at each other. In the American Civil War,* men used natural cover,

* American Civil War: a war (1861–65) between the north and the south of the country

or dug holes in the ground. We might think of this as the first modern war, in the way that men fought, and in the numbers who died. More than half a million people were killed.

The machine gun

In the year after the war began, a new and even more terrible type of gun was invented. It had ten barrels, which were turned by a handle and could fire 200 bullets a minute. Richard Gatling, an American doctor, first thought of it, and it was called the machine gun.

Twenty years later, an American called Hiram Maxim was living in London when another American suggested a way for him to get rich. He said that Maxim should invent something that allowed Europeans to kill each other more easily. Maxim's answer was a machine gun with one barrel. Every time a bullet was fired, the hot gas was used to pull the next one into position. It could fire 300 bullets a minute.

In the first years, though, the Maxim gun wasn't used against Europeans, but mainly against Africans. The Maxim gun and the repeating rifle allowed small numbers of soldiers to defend themselves against large numbers of fighters who had little equipment. Until this time, European control of Africa had been mainly limited to areas near the coast. It was too expensive in money and lives to try to take the more central areas using single-shot guns. Now things changed. In 1879, a force of Zulus had killed over 1,300 British soldiers at Isandlwana, in southern Africa. Only fifteen years later, during the Matabele War, fifty soldiers with four Maxim guns successfully defended themselves against 5,000 Ndebele. At Omdurman, in 1898, Maxim guns played their part in the killing of 11,000 men in exchange for just twenty-eight British lives. The writer Hilaire Belloc described the hard new reality when he wrote:

Whatever happens, we have got
The Maxim gun, and they have not.

The new repeating rifles and the Maxim gun meant that quite small numbers of soldiers were able to win battles in Africa. In the last years of the nineteenth century, the European countries raced to take control of the continent. This, and another race to get more modern guns, led to the beginning of the First World War in 1914.

The race also meant building bigger and bigger warships, but when the war came, most of the ships stayed at home. Neither side was willing to send them out; if they were lost, the country would be defenseless. Instead, the war was fought on land, and great numbers were killed by repeating rifles, machine guns, and cannon.

On 1 July 1916, the British Army attacked the Germans along the River Somme in France. By the end of the day, over 19,000 of its men were dead, and no real progress had been made. This was the high point—or low point—of the power of the gun. Since then, improvements in army vehicles and air power have meant that the advantage isn't always with the defenders.

Chapter 5   Engines

Until about 300 years ago, power came from the wind, from water, or from the strength of humans and animals. Using these forms of power, machines were built and people sailed around the world. But the invention of the steam engine was the real start of the modern age.

The steam engine

In the first century, the inventor Hero of Alexandria described a ball with two jets. When the ball was filled with steam, the jets

Hero's steam engine

made it turn round and round. A model of this was made quite recently. It turned 1,500 times a minute. The problem, though, is that this kind of machine only works well at high speed. Hero liked to make mechanical toys to entertain people, and it is possible that he used this machine to power some of these. It is unlikely that it had any other uses. A number of other writers in later centuries suggested ideas for better steam engines, but it took some time before anyone made one that actually worked.

In 1690, the Frenchman Denis Papin wrote a description of a steam engine. He then actually built one and it was used to lift water up to a higher level. In Papin's engine, water inside a tube was heated until it turned into steam and pushed up a round metal plate. When this reached its highest point, cold water hit the outside of the tube. This turned the steam inside back into water. Water takes less space than steam, and the fall in pressure, with the pressure of the outside air, pulled the metal plate down again.

In 1698, the English engineer Thomas Savery built a steam engine that used two metal containers. Steam was put into each of these in turn. When cold water hit the container from the outside, the steam turned into water again and the change in pressure could be used to lift up more water. Savery's engine, though, could only lift water a few meters without using pressures which might cause an explosion.

In England in 1712, Thomas Newcomen, independently of Papin, had drawn plans for a steam engine. In his engine, the steam was heated separately before it was introduced into the tube at low pressure. The round metal plate was connected to a long piece of wood and the other end of the piece of wood lifted water. The weight of the other end made the metal plate go up; when the water turned into steam, the fall in pressure pulled it down again.

Since the tubes in Newcomen's engine, as in Papin's, had to be heated and cooled repeatedly, it could only operate twelve times

Newcomen's steam engine

a minute. Like other engines before it, it was only useful for lifting water. It was widely used by 1725, though, and continued to be used for sixty years, in Britain and in a number of other countries.

James Watt

In Glasgow in 1763, the 28-year-old instrument maker James Watt was given a model of a Newcomen steam engine to repair. This model was used by the University of Glasgow for teaching. While he was working on it, he thought about ways to improve it. The idea came to him on a Sunday afternoon in 1765, during a walk in the local park. He realized that if the steam was turned back into water in a separate tube, the main tube could be kept hot. This greatly increased the speed of the engine. At the same time, it reduced problems caused by repeatedly heating and cooling the tube. Watt's new engine was four times more powerful than Newcomen's.

Until 1774, cannon were made with a hole down the middle, which meant that there might be some weaknesses in the barrel. In that year, the Englishman John Wilkinson invented a machine for cutting out the center of a cannon. James Watt had been very worried about the escape of steam from his tubes because they didn't fit round the metal plates tightly enough. The two men started working together, and Wilkinson's new machine was used in the production of Watt's engines.

Within a few years, Watt had built an engine that introduced steam both above and below the metal plate, allowing a double action. He continued to try different ideas, and in 1781 he produced a new engine. Unlike his earlier engines, where the movement was up and down, this one could be used to make wheels turn. Until that time, factories had to use horses or water power to make their machines work. Now, one of Watt's engines could do the job, and do it better. It was soon used in many factories.

Although he was responsible for moving ideas forward in a number of ways, Watt can also be blamed for slowing progress down. In 1755, he had been given the right to stop anyone else making a steam engine like his. For the next twenty-five years, his company made almost all steam engines, and Watt charged his customers a lot of money for using one of them.

He compared his machine to a horse, which, he said, could pull a weight of eighty-two kilograms. So a machine might be, for example, a twenty-horsepower engine. Watt worked out how much money each company saved by using his machine instead of a team of horses. The company then had to pay him one-third of this amount every year for the next twenty-five years. When James Watt died in 1819, he was a very rich man.

High-pressure steam

All of Watt's engines used low-pressure steam. He always refused to make high-pressure engines because he was afraid of explosions. The move into high-pressure steam was made at about the same time by two men, Richard Trevithick in England and Oliver Evans in the US. Evans had begun to work on his high-pressure steam engine in 1773, at the age of eighteen. In 1789, he invented the first steam-powered land vehicle. It is possible that Trevithick borrowed his ideas from Evans, but Evans never said so, and it is more likely that he had the same ideas independently.

Trevithick came from Cornwall, in the southwest of England, and his most successful engine was called "the Cornish engine." He was also the first man to build a working railroad engine, in 1804. This could move at six kilometers an hour. His example was followed by George Stephenson, who built one in 1815. Ten years later, Stephenson's engines ran at a record speed of twenty-five kilometers an hour between Stockton and Darlington in the north of England. This was the first railroad to carry passengers on regular schedules. Stephenson's engine, the Rocket, pulled twenty-one passenger cars containing 450 passengers.

Steam was used to power boats and ships from the very early days. The first steamboat traveled up the River Saône, in France, in 1783. By the end of the nineteenth century, the world depended on steamships for moving things from country to country and for defense.

Although a number of steam-powered road vehicles had been built during the nineteenth century, their great weight had meant that they were mainly limited to farm work. At the end of the nineteenth century, although steam was used to power trains, ships, and factories, local travel still depended on the horse. In fact, the number of horses in London at the time had become a great problem; hundreds of men worked to clean the streets that they passed through.

Gasoline and jet engines

Human progress needed a new idea, and it appeared as the gasoline engine. In a steam engine, a fire heated water to produce power. In this new engine, the gasoline itself was lit inside the tube. The French engineer Alphonse Beau de Rochas first had the idea, in 1862. In Germany, Nikolaus Otto turned the idea into a working engine. Otto sold around 35,000 of his engines in the next ten years, and by that time other German engineers had built better ones.

Gottlieb Daimler had worked in Otto's factory from the early 1870s and had helped him with his new engine. In 1882, he left and started his own company with Wilhelm Maybach, and in three years they built a modern, lightweight gasoline engine. In 1885, Daimler produced the first motorcycle to test it, but Karl Benz had built a gasoline-driven car by the same year. Daimler and Maybach showed their car a year later. In 1892, Rudolf Diesel invented a different kind of engine. This used a heavier kind of oil, which lit under pressure. His idea was especially useful for heavy ship or factory engines.

Frank Whittle joined the British air force at the age of sixteen. He became a fighter pilot, a test pilot, and then spent 1934–37 at Cambridge University studying mechanical sciences. He realized the need for a very fast airplane which could use the thinner air higher in the sky. By 1930, he had invented a jet engine. Like the gasoline engine, this burned gasoline and air, but instead of using the power to make a propeller turn, it sent the hot gas straight out behind the airplane to push it forward.

The government didn't seem interested in his idea, so Whittle started a company, Power Jets Limited, in 1936. The first engine was ready for testing the following year. The beginning of the Second World War changed the government's attitude and Whittle's first jet airplane, the Gloster E28/39, flew in May 1941. It reached a top speed of 600 kilometers an hour and a height of 7,500 meters.

In Germany, Hans Joachim Pabst von Ohain had built a jet engine in 1935, but he received more government support and had his first jet—the Heinkel He 178—in the skies earlier than the British machine. On 19 July 1942, the Messerschmitt 262 took off. This was the world's first jet-powered fighter. The first British jet was used by the British air force in 1944.

Progress was slower in Germany because of engine problems with the Messerschmitt 262. In the end, around 1,430 airplanes were built, and they appeared in the skies over Germany in the final months of the war. They were very fast but could only fly for a short time, and they made no difference to the result of the war. But the new knowledge in both countries was useful in the following years. Since then, jet engines have been used to fly people around the world in greater and greater numbers.

Chapter 6   Flight

For many centuries, people watched birds and dreamed that they could fly. We cannot fly like birds, though; we don't have enough strength in our arms to move wings up and down. We also really need the power of an engine to drive us forward. Many people died learning these lessons, before controlled flight became possible.

Flying machines

In the year 875 in Cordoba, Spain, a man called Abbas Ibn Firnas built a flying machine which could carry a human being. He invited the people of the town to come and watch as he jumped off a mountain. Reports tell us that he flew some distance, but the landing was hard. Abbas hurt his back badly and was never able to fly again. He said later that he hadn't noticed that birds land on their tails—he had forgotten to put a tail on the machine.

It is possible that news of his flight reached England, carried there by men returning from war in the Middle East. Whether this is true or not, in 1010 a man called Oliver jumped off a church roof in Malmesbury. This time we know the distance of his flight—125 steps. He was only a little luckier than Abbas; he broke both his legs, but he too was never able to fly again.

In the last years of the fifteenth century, the Italian Leonardo da Vinci studied the flight of birds and made a number of drawings of flying machines. His early machines tried to copy the movement of birds' wings, which he didn't fully understand. But less than ten years before his death in 1519, he drew a machine with wings that didn't move. One of these machines was built recently, and it did fly, although it was too dangerous to be tested without ropes holding it to the ground. In 1536 in France, Denis Bolor returned to the idea of moving wings. He tried to fly using wings that were moved up and down. The idea didn't work and he fell to his death.

The most successful of these early flights was in 1638 in Istanbul. Hezarfen Celebi built a pair of wings using da Vinci's drawings. He made nine practice flights from the top of a hill. When he was sure that the wings would work, he jumped off a high building in Galata and flew across the Bosphorus to land in the market place at Uskudar (Scutari). The government gave him 1,000 gold pieces, but it was frightened of Celebi's powers and sent him to live in Algeria.

Balloons

Another way of flying was tried in France in 1783, when the Montgolfier brothers sent up a hot-air balloon. To make the hot air, they burned wool and old shoes. Later that same year, they tested their new idea in front of King Louis XVI. This time the balloon carried passengers: two birds and a sheep. The first manned flight was in November, when two men in a balloon reached a height of twenty-five meters. The following month, the first flight with one person was made by Jacques Charles. He went up to 3,500 meters and flew for over thirty-six kilometers. In January 1784 one of the Montgolfier brothers, Joseph, finally flew, with six other passengers. A year later, a balloon crossed the water between France and England. The trip took two and a half hours.

Powered flight

Unfortunately, you can't control the direction that a balloon flies in. The Frenchman Henri Giffard tried to solve this in the middle of the nineteenth century. He built a long balloon, known as an airship, which was powered by a steam engine. It flew twenty-seven kilometers west from Paris to Trappes.

In 1890 another Frenchman, Clément Ader, flew a steam-powered airplane for fifty meters near Paris. Although this was the first powered flight of an airplane, it mainly showed that steam engines were too heavy for the job. True flight only became possible with the arrival of the lighter gasoline engine.

At the beginning of the twentieth century, two American bicycle mechanics, Wilbur and Orville Wright, used a gasoline engine when they built their flying machine. On 17 December 1903, this lifted into the sky at Kittyhawk, North Carolina, at 10:35 A.M. Orville was at the controls. The flight only lasted twelve seconds, but it was the first powered, manned, heavier-than-air controlled flight.

The Wright bothers built a second machine, but their total flying time in 1904 was only forty-five minutes. Then they learned how to turn the airplane, and in October 1905 they made a flight that covered thirty-nine kilometers in thirty-eight minutes and three seconds.

One of the Wright brothers' planes—the "Flyer"

In the next few years, flying progressed very quickly. Louis Bleriot became the first person to fly an airplane from France to England in 1909. Worried about war, all sides began to look at the possible uses of airplanes. At the beginning of the war, airplanes were mainly used for watching the positions of enemy soldiers. Soon, though, there were hundreds on each side of the front line.

At first, fighting between machines was limited to guns in the hands of the pilots. Early German two-seater machines were flown by a pilot who carried an officer with a rifle, but soon the officers started to fly the airplane themselves.

Because of the problem of firing a machine gun through a propeller, the first fighter airplanes were two-seaters. These either had a moveable gun behind the pilot, or a propeller behind and a gunner in front. Then, in 1915, the Dutch engineer Anthony Fokker, who owned a factory in Germany, invented a machine to time the gun so it could fire through a front propeller. The new single-seater Fokker fighter had a great advantage and shot down many airplanes until the British and French were able to copy his idea.

Although parachutes existed—the first jump, from a balloon, had been made in 1797—neither side was willing to give them to pilots. British commanders said that if pilots had a parachute, they might jump out at the first sign of trouble. It is also possible that there was another reason. If the British gave parachutes to their pilots, the Germans might do the same. And since most fighting between airplanes took place on the German side of the lines, the Germans would get their shot-down pilots back while the British wouldn't.

In the First World War, airships were also used for fighting. The first flight of the German machine, the Zeppelin, had taken place in 1900, and there were 159 attacks on Britain using airships of this type, during which 557 people were killed. They did little real damage, but forced the British to keep many fighter airplanes at home to defend the country.

Flying around the world

After the war, the airship was seen as the future of passenger travel, but after the crash of the British R101 in France in 1930, Britain stopped using them. Germany continued until 1937, when the *Hindenburg* was destroyed by fire at Lakehurst, New Jersey, and thirty-six people lost their lives.

During the 1920s and 1930s, airplanes flew further and further. The Atlantic Ocean was crossed in 1919 by two British officers, John Alcock and Albert Brown. They took off from Newfoundland, Canada, in a Vickers bomber and landed in the west of Ireland sixteen hours and twenty-seven minutes later. It was a difficult flight, some of the time through fog and snow. Brown had to climb out onto the wings four times to cut ice from the engines.

Eight years later, Charles Lindbergh made the first flight by one person, in an airplane called *The Spirit of St. Louis*. The following year another American, Amelia Earhart, became the first woman to fly across the ocean, although, as she said herself, she was really a passenger on an airplane flown by two men. She did it alone, though, in May 1932. She was the first woman to fly across the Atlantic alone, and she was the first person to do it alone since Lindbergh. Earhart made a number of other long-distance flights before she was lost over the Pacific in 1937 while she was trying to fly around the world.

War and peace

In September 1923, US airplanes had bombed the old warships *Virginia* and *New Jersey* as a test. Both had been sunk within a few minutes. During the war, the usefulness of air power was shown time after time until all countries learned that warships needed airplanes to protect them, and that the most important ship was now one that could carry airplanes. The war between the US and Japan in the Pacific was fought between carriers that never went near each other.

In the Second World War, bombing was used in a new and terrible way. Many cities were burned, and a new type of bomb was dropped on Hiroshima and Nagasaki, in Japan, in 1946.

After this war, people looked again at the peaceful uses of air power, and in the 1950s and 60s air travel became possible for more and more people. The de Havilland Comet, which first flew in 1952, was the first airplane built especially to carry passengers. But after three crashes in two years, it was taken out of the air. Its square windows led to weaknesses in the body of the airplane. Although later Comets with round windows flew, the most popular airplanes by that time were built by the American companies Boeing and Douglas.

In 1969, Britain and France produced the Concorde, the first passenger airplane to fly faster than the speed of sound. Many people thought that the future had arrived, but the real change had happened two years earlier when the slower but enormous Boeing 747s began to fly. People realized that it was too expensive, noisy, and dirty to fly faster than the speed of sound. The future for passenger travel was increasing numbers of slower flights.

The first helicopter had been flown in 1907, when Paul Cornu, a French inventor, built a machine that stayed thirty centimeters off the ground for twenty seconds. Then in 1939, the Russian Igor Sikorsky built a usable machine. It stayed up over an airport in Stratford, Connecticut, for one hour and five minutes in 1941, piloted by Sikorsky himself. Little progress was made with helicopters in the Second World War, although they were used greatly in later wars in Korea and Vietnam. In the world today, helicopters have a large number of peacetime uses—as air ambulances, for police work and traffic control, as well as for travel.

The first rocket to actually fly and work was the German V2, first fired against England in September 1944. V2s continued to land on southern England until March of the following year, when the British army reached the part of Germany they were fired from. A number of German V2 scientists later worked for the American and Russian space programs. In March 1946, the first American-built rocket reached a height of eighty kilometers, and in 1961 Yuri Gagarin became the first human being to travel in space when he flew once around the Earth.

The space race, as it was called, continued through the 1960s; both the United States and the Soviet Union sent up better and better rockets. In time, the Americans passed the Russians and on 20 July 1969, Neil Armstrong became the first person to walk on the moon.

The space program slowed down after this, although a space station, *Skylab*, was sent up in 1973. Eight years later, *Columbia* became the first vehicle to go into space and return to Earth. In 2004, *Rover Spirit* successfully landed on Mars. Americans plan to return human beings to the moon by 2020; these people will, they hope, build a scientific station and prepare to travel to Mars. At one time, people used to say, "The sky's the limit." These days, this isn't true.

Chapter 7   Communication

Before 1860, it could take six weeks for a letter to travel from New York to California. Letters were taken by boat to Panama, then carried overland to another boat, which took them north. Californians joked that events were forgotten on the East Coast before they were known on the West Coast. But this situation began to change—and to change quickly.

Moving arms

In 1791, the Frenchman Claude Chappe invented a new method of signaling. He put up tall buildings in long lines. At the top of each building were arms which could be moved into different positions. Each position meant a different letter, from A to Z. This worked in daylight and when you could see for quite a long way.

In 1794, news reached Paris by this method that the Prussians had taken the town of Conde-sur-l'Escaut, 145 kilometers away, in less than an hour. By 1852, there were 556 of these buildings in France and 250 more in the rest of Europe. Chappe, though, wasn't happy. He had hoped for much more much sooner, and he killed himself in 1805. The stone with his name and dates on it shows two wooden arms in the "at rest" position.

In 1790 people in Philadelphia, US, began to buy and sell parts of companies. Shortly after this, a group of businessmen in Philadelphia put up a line of these stations between the city and New York to communicate prices. The stations also used the sun and mirrors. If the sun was shining, information could travel between the two cities in ten minutes.

The electric telegraph

Between 3 April 1860 and 24 October 1861, horses carried mail

Various positions of the Machine.

A Chappe semaphore tower

between St Joseph, Missouri, and Sacramento, California. At a cost of one dollar for fourteen grams, letters and packages could be carried 3,000 kilometers through the six states between Missouri and California and arrive within ten days. Although the service never made money for its owners, its story is still told. It all came to an end in 1861 when the Pacific Telegraph line was completed. After that, messages got through very quickly, although letters took more time until the railroad to California opened in 1869.

The beginnings of electric telegraphy go back to the early nineteenth century, but the first working system was invented by the Englishmen William Cooke and Charles Wheatstone in 1837. This used five needles, which pointed to different letters on a board. By 1843, the two men had built a connection along the railroad between Paddington in central London and Slough, thirty-five kilometers to the west. Two years later, this was very useful when a murderer was seen getting on a train at Paddington. A message was telegraphed to Slough and the police were waiting for him when he arrived.

In 1837 the Americans Samuel Morse, an artist with an interest in telegraphy, and Alfred Vail, an engineer, invented a new way to signal letters and words. The telegraph made immediate use of this. Now, instead of moving needles, the operator used a simple key to send long and short sounds. At the other end, these sounds were printed onto a piece of paper as long and short lines and then had to be written out in normal language. In 1855, David Hughes invented a printing telegraph; after that, the message was simply typed at one end of the line and printed in words at the other end.

In 1851, Britain—which already had 6,400 kilometers of telegraph line—was connected with France, and in 1858 with the US. But the wire across the Atlantic Ocean was too thin and it failed within a week. Another wire, put down in 1865, was still too thin and also broke. A successful connection was completed the following year. By the 1870s, Europe and America were connected to India, the Far East, and Australia.

Progress in communication affected many areas of life. In Aachen, Germany, in 1849, Paul Julius Reuter started an organization for sending business information. He started to sell news reports as well, and his company, Reuters, still does this today, all around the world. In the Crimean War of 1853–56, a wire was put in place across the Black Sea from Balaclava to Varna in Bulgaria. This allowed British and French commanders to contact their governments using the existing European system.

The telephone

Ordinary people could also use the telegraph for urgent messages, but these had to be short and impersonal. This changed in 1876, when the telephone was invented, allowing people to communicate in a more human way. Although there are a number of possible inventors, most people believe that the person responsible was Alexander Graham Bell. He was born in Edinburgh, Scotland, but the family moved to the United States when he was twenty-three. Both his mother and wife were deaf, and his father was a speech teacher, so Bell had a lifelong interest in speech. "Mr. Watson, come here, I want you," were the first words he spoke on the telephone. They weren't meant to be sent, but Bell was working on one end of the system while his assistant was listening in another room.

The first telephone exchange opened in New Haven, Connecticut, with twenty-one customers. In Europe, Bell increased interest in the telephone with a number of talks, including one that he gave to Queen Victoria in 1878. In the same year, the first company was formed in Britain. It is interesting, though, that Bell always refused to have a telephone in his own home.

At the beginning, all telephone connections were made by operators in the exchange, and this gave acceptable employment to women. After 1899, it was possible to connect using numbers on the phone, but the women were paid very little and their bosses saw no reason to change in a hurry. The Bell Company didn't use the new system until after the First World War.

The first international telephone line connected Paris and Brussels in 1887. By 1900, international services were being connected as well as local ones. This meant putting more wires under the ocean. Britain was connected to the continent of Europe in 1891. Although existing telegraph wires could be used, long-distance telephones needed stations to make the sound stronger along the line. New York wasn't connected to San Francisco until 1915. A radio connection between London and New York was made in 1927, although this depended on weather conditions. Similar connections were made to Australia and South America in 1930, and from that time the telephone was truly a world service, although it was expensive. Connections using wire took longer; the first one across the Atlantic Ocean wasn't in place until 1956.

The telephone didn't become common in private houses until the 1920s and even then, only for the middle and upper classes. Since that time, it has reached everybody in the world's richer countries. People used to have one phone in the hall, for use on important occasions, but many now have phones in the kitchen, the living room, the bedroom—even, in some houses, the bathroom.

In the 1980s, cell phones appeared. The first ones were very big, and young business people wore special suits with a deep pocket to hold them. Now they are hand-sized and very common, although—strangely—fewer Americans own them than Europeans or Japanese.

It has always been difficult to build telephone lines in poorer countries. Because it is now easier to build a system to make cell phones work, it is possible that in some parts of the world telephone lines will never be built.

Radio

There were limits to the usefulness of the telephone. Ships were out of contact, and all places needed connections and exchanges. In 1894 a Brazilian, Roberto Landell de Moura, sent a radio signal in São Paulo. He worked for the Roman Catholic Church and the Church didn't like this new invention. He was told to stop work on it, and the following year some angry people burned down the building where he worked. Five years passed before Landell was able to show his invention again. By this time, the leader in radio was the Italian Guglielmo Marconi.

When he was only twenty years old, Marconi had done his first work with radio on his family's land near Bologna. By 1895, he had succeeded in sending messages, using the Morse system, for two and a half kilometers. At the other end of the line, his brother fired a hunting rifle to show that they had been received.

Marconi received no support in Italy, so he went to London, where he succeeded in interesting the Post Office. He formed his own company in 1897, and two years later sent a message to France. By 1901, he had sent one across the Atlantic from Poldhu in Cornwall to St John's, Newfoundland. This was surprising, since the world is round and radio waves travel in straight lines. The answer came in 1924, when it was discovered that the radio waves were sent back to Earth from high up in the sky.

In 1909, Marconi received the Nobel Prize. By that time over 300 ships were using radio signals and there was already a public service across the Atlantic. In 1904, the Cunard ship *Campania* had begun to print the daily news for passengers. In 1910, while it was sailing from Belgium to Canada, its captain read the daily news report and realized that the murderer Dr. Crippen was on the ship. He didn't tell the other passengers—so millions of people around the world knew, but not them. The police were waiting for Dr. Crippen when he arrived in Canada.

When the *Titanic* sank in 1912, the two "Marconi men" on the ship, Jack Phillips and Harold Bride, stayed and sent messages until the power failed. Bride lived, but Phillips went down with the ship. Their signals, using Marconi's invention, brought the *SS Carpathia* to the scene to save 712 people from the ocean.

The early messages were sent across the Atlantic using Morse's system. With better equipment, speech was first sent from Virginia to Paris in 1915. After the First World War, public broadcasting increased greatly. By 1922 there were 600 broadcasting stations, and when the BBC was started in 1927 there were already two million radios in Britain.

Television

It is difficult to say who invented television. Unlike some other new ideas, which suddenly came to one person, people had talked about the possibility of *television*, or "long-distance sight," since Marconi invented the radio. The three possible inventors are John Logie Baird from Scotland; Vladimir Kosmo Zworykin, who grew up in Russia but did his work in the United States, and Philo Taylor Farnsworth, who came from Utah in the US.

Zworykin is usually seen as the father of TV because he invented an electronic tube in 1923. John Logie Baird was the first to send a simple television picture across a few meters, in 1924. He showed his new invention in Selfridges department store in London the following year. The pictures, though, were of very poor quality.

Farnsworth was the first to send good pictures. He did this in 1927, using a tube he had built himself. Zworykin wasn't able to

45

do the same until 1934, although Farnsworth's camera needed too much light, and Zworykin's method was better in the end. The BBC bought Baird's system and began regular test broadcasts in 1929. They also tested an electronic system invented by Marconi. In 1937, the BBC decided that the Marconi system was the way forward and stopped using Baird's system.

Zworykin and Farnsworth each worked for a different company, and at around this time these companies fought in the US courts about who invented television. Farnsworth's company won the case, and we should probably think of him as the real inventor of TV.

The first person to invent color TV was either the Mexican Guillermo González Camarena, or the Hungarian, Peter Goldmark, who worked in the US. Most Mexicans will say it was González, but Americans—and Hungarians—say that it was Goldmark. It is often like this with inventions.

Both men produced quite similar systems in 1940; they used turning circles colored red, blue, and yellow. Unfortunately for Goldmark, he worked for the CBS company, but most televisions at the time were made by another company, RCA, and these couldn't use Goldmark's system. RCA had plans for color television too, but they weren't ready at the time. When the company did introduce color, in 1954, they used their own electronic system. González started the first television station in Mexico and later sold television equipment to the US. Strangely, both men were killed in car crashes, González in 1965 and Goldmark twelve years later.

In recent years, computers and the Internet have changed the way we communicate.

Chapter 8   Computers

Not long ago, all letters were written by hand or on typewriters, and information was held mainly in libraries. Affordable personal computers only appeared in the 1980s, followed by the Internet and e-mail a few years later. It is easy to forget how recent these inventions are.

Charles Babbage

In 1943, Thomas J. Watson, who started the company IBM, said that he thought there was a world market for about five computers. He was very wrong. There are now over 100 million *personal* computers in use around the world—as well as the bigger computers used by large organizations.

In 1822, in England, Charles Babbage began work on a counting machine. He was given £1,500 of government money to complete the job, and worked on it for the next ten years. This became known as the Difference Engine Number 1. The government's patience finally ended in 1834, when Babbage still hadn't finished building it, but had planned the first programmable computer. This included programs (written using cards with holes in them), a reader which was able to get results from the information, and a memory—all the things that were found in later computers.

Babbage asked the government for money to make the new machine, but was refused. He then built the Difference Engine Number 2. At two meters high, this was a slightly smaller and much simpler model that used only a small number of the 25,000 parts in the first machine. In 1991, one hundred years after Babbage's death, a copy was built using his plans. It did what Babbage said it would do. Babbage wasn't recognized in his lifetime. Very few people knew about his work and most of them weren't interested.

Early computers

Later in the nineteenth century, in the US, Herman Hollerith also used cards with holes when he invented a machine to count government figures more quickly. The 1880 population count had taken eight years, and people were worried that the 1890 one would take even longer. Hollerith's machine, which used electricity to read, sort, and count the cards, did the job in a year.

The English mathematician Alan Turing led the move toward a machine that was able to "think" in a real way. He wrote a paper which is the real start of the computer age, about a machine that read and wrote information, with a memory to hold it in, a central processor, and a program of mathematical commands. This became known as a "Turing machine."

During the Second World War, Turing worked on reading secret German messages. The work also included the building of a simple computer. After the war, he used his knowledge of mathematics to write the first programming languages.

In Germany, Konrad Zuse started work on his first mechanical computer in 1934, but two years later he changed to electrical connections. In 1940, the war interrupted the building of his third computer, but after a year he left the army and completed the Z3, an electrical machine which was controlled by a program. The German air force helped him, and the Z3 was used to help build airplanes and the V2 rockets. At the end of the war, Zuse's latest machine was taken to Switzerland to be finished. This was the Z4, the first fully-programmable computer. It had a mechanical memory of 1,024 words.

From large machines to small

The first of the modern all-electronic computers was the ENIAC, built at the University of Pennsylvania. It was begun in

1943 and used by the US army. It was 150 square meters in size and needed an enormous quantity of electricity. It also became very hot, and this was a great problem.

The first computer for business use, the UNIVAC 1, was also used to count population. It became famous when it said that Dwight D. Eisenhower would win the race to become president in 1952. Its operators refused to believe this and reprogrammed it for a more likely result. When Eisenhower won easily, somebody said, "The problem with machines is people."

In the late 1950s, the transistor was invented. This was cheaper, smaller, and worked better than the old electronic connections. In 1958, Jack St. Clair Kilby of Texas Instruments had the idea of putting a few transistors together on a board. Today, hundreds of thousands of electronic parts can be put together on a board that is no more than one centimeter square.

The Colossus computer (in use in Britain from 1944)

In 1971, the Intel 4004 processor appeared. The central working part of the computer was now brought together in something that you could hold in your hand. Gordon Moore, who started Intel, said in 1965 that the power of processors would double every twelve months for the next ten years. This was changed to eighteen months in 1975, and since then "Moore's Law" has continued to be true.

In 1965, US engineer Kenneth Olsen produced the PDP-8. This was a machine about the size of two televisions and it sold for $18,000, much less than the $1,000,000 cost of larger computers. It was a great success with scientists and engineers.

The first three personal computers appeared in 1977. The best of these was the Apple II. Two years before, Stephen Wozniak had built and marketed the Apple 1. This had no case, all the electronics could be seen, and it was only for serious computer hobbyists. Wozniak's friend Steve Jobs asked him to build a machine that more people could use. The result was the Apple II, which sold for $1,298.

Among a number of computer hobbyists in California were Bill Gates and Paul Allen, who started Micro-Soft (later Microsoft). IBM, which had seen the success of the Apple II, was interested in selling its own machine. Microsoft was given the job of writing the operating system. IBM could use this system, but not own it, so Microsoft received $10 for every copy sold. IBM had failed to realize that systems, not machines, were going to make money in the future. This was possibly the biggest mistake in the history of computers.

Large numbers of companies produced copies of IBM machines, but every machine—about 30 million in the 1980s—used Microsoft systems. The power of IBM meant that business followed its lead, and the Apple machines were mainly bought by home users or by people who needed good drawing systems.

In 1971, IBM produced the first floppy disk. This came in a

paper packet and was twenty centimeters wide, but it was still a great improvement on the tapes that had been used before. The modern nine-centimeter disk was first produced by Sony in 1981.

The Internet

In 1969, several university and government computers were connected together by the US Department of Defense, so scientists in different parts of the world could share information and work together. Two years after this, a program for sending electronic mail ("e-mail") was written. The first international connection was made in 1973 between University College London and Norway. Queen Elizabeth II of the United Kingdom sent her first e-mail in 1976. Three years later, the University of Essex built a system which allowed a number of users to exchange information at the same time. In 1982, the word "Internet" was invented to describe this.

In 1989 Philip Emeagwali, who came from Nigeria but worked in the US, connected 65,536 separate computer processors to work together and perform 3,100,000,000 mathematical operations every second. These were used in the search to find oil.

Two years later, the Englishman Tim Berners-Lee invented a new system. This made it possible to find and read documents without knowing where they actually were, and it became known as the "World Wide Web." It appeared on the Internet in 1991, starting an explosion of information. For the next two years, use of the Internet grew at around 341,000% each year.

The ability of computers to do difficult mathematics and the power of the Internet to help people communicate with each other have made it possible to improve ideas much faster than before. All the more recent inventions in this book have been helped by computers.

Chapter 9   Ideas

Can you imagine yourself as an inventor? You might think that you need to know a lot of science, but this isn't always true. The most important thing is a new idea, and ideas can come to all kinds of people in many different situations. Some of these ideas have changed the world.

Catseyes™ ★

A simple idea can sometimes make millions of dollars for the inventor if enough copies of the invention are sold. In 1933, an English road builder called Percy Shaw was driving home. At one point on the road there was a bend with a steep drop on the right. The night was foggy, and Shaw followed the road with difficulty. Suddenly, the lights of his car caught a cat sitting on a fence. The light shone back to him clearly from the animal's eyes and possibly saved his life.

Shaw realized that "glass eyes" down the center of roads could help to guide drivers. He started work and put together glass balls and mirrors inside a rubber case. Each time a car drove over them, the "eyes" sank into the road and were cleaned by a piece of rubber. The government didn't show much interest in Shaw's idea until his "Catseyes" became useful during the war years because street lamps were switched off at night and cars had to use very weak lights. Enemy airplanes couldn't see the light from Catseyes.

After the war, the government started a program to put Catseyes on all Britain's roads. Shaw became rich, but continued to live in the same house. In most ways his life didn't change.

★ ™: a sign showing that the name is owned by a person or company that makes them, and cannot be used by others

Post-it™ notes

A new idea can sometimes have an unexpected use. In the 1970s Art Fry, who worked for a company called 3M, was looking for a new way to mark his place in his Bible. He noticed that somebody at the company had produced a new type of sticky material. It was strong enough to hold onto paper, but could be lifted off easily and left nothing behind. He realized that his problem was solved. 3M liked the idea and started to make little books of yellow squares of paper with this sticky material along one side. They were called Post-it notes, although most people today call them "yellow stickies."

Velcro™

Sometimes inventors only have to copy what already exists in nature. In 1948 George de Mestral, a Swiss mountain climber and inventor, returned from a walk with his dog. Both he and the animal were covered in sticky balls from plants. Looking at these closely, he saw how they caught hold of the cloth, and an idea was born. He decided to call his new material Velcro and in time his company was selling 55 million meters of it every year. Today, Velcro is used on clothes and bags to keep pockets shut and to hold pieces of cloth together.

Lock-nuts

There are times when ideas come from looking at things in a new way. Catherine Ryan noticed that it was difficult to take her wedding ring off because her finger grew bigger when she pulled. She thought of a new kind of nut. It would get tighter as it was turned and so stay in place. Today these are called lock-nuts. Millions of them are used in the building of many types of machines. Before Catherine Ryan had her idea, another nut had to be tightened against the first one. This took longer and cost more.

The sewing machine

Dreams can sometimes give an answer when deep thought has failed. In 1845, Elias Howe was sitting at his desk, trying to turn his idea for a sewing machine into something that might work. He fell asleep and dreamed he was in Africa and had been caught by local people who weren't very friendly. In fact, they were going to eat him. They put him in a pot of water and started to heat it. He kept trying to climb out of the pot, but they pushed him back with their sharp spears.

When he woke up, he thought about his dream. He remembered that the point of each spear had a hole in it and realized that this was the answer to his problem. Howe's machine was never very successful, but the first popular machine, invented by Isaac Singer in 1851, used Howe's needle with a hole in the pointed end. Howe took Singer to court and won. He collected $5 for every sewing machine made in America, and became the fourth richest man in the country.

The windshield wiper

From time to time the answer comes from somebody who is new to a situation. In 1903, on a trip to New York City, Mary Anderson of Alabama watched as a driver got out of his streetcar many times to brush snow from the glass at the front. Millions of people had seen the same thing on many occasions, but Anderson made a simple drawing of a long piece of rubber that could clean the glass. This was moved backward and forward by hand from inside. By 1916, these were being fitted to all American cars, and they were later powered by electricity.

A new vacuum cleaner

Sometimes no improvements are made to a machine until somebody asks a simple question—why? In 1978, vacuum cleaners hadn't really changed very much since the beginning of the century. There had been a number of improvements, but air was still pulled through a paper bag and in time this didn't work so well because of the dust. One day, James Dyson found that he had no more vacuum cleaner bags. He took the old one out of the trash can, and discovered that it wasn't really full. He shook the dust out of it, but it still didn't work well.

Dyson started to think about a better method. On the roof of a local factory, there was a machine to remove dust from the air; it turned very fast and caught the dust against its sides. Dyson visited the factory that night and made several drawings of the machine. He rushed home and made a model out of card, which he fitted to his vacuum cleaner. It had no bag. Instead, a part of the machine inside turned round very fast. The dust hit the sides of this and fell to the bottom of the machine. To Dyson's surprise, it worked well. It took fourteen years, though, and more than 5,000 models, before the Dual Cyclone (DC01) appeared in stores in 1993. It became the most popular vacuum cleaner in the UK, and Dyson cleaners are best-sellers in Western Europe.

A radio for Africa

Human need often leads to change. In 1991, Trevor Bayliss saw a television program about Africa. A medical worker said that if more people were able to listen to the radio, advice on disease control could be broadcast. But many areas were without electricity and batteries were expensive, often costing more than a week's food for a family. Bayliss had a new idea for a radio. You turned a handle a number of times and this produced enough

Bayliss's radio

electricity to make it work. It took some time, though, to produce a working model and to make companies believe in the idea.

Then, in 1994, Bayliss's latest model, which ran for fourteen minutes, appeared on *Tomorrow's World*, a BBC program about inventions. After this, he got the money to finish the job. His radio is now supplied to many people in the poorer parts of the world. It is also sold at full cost in Europe and the US, where people like it because used batteries damage the Earth.

One of the first inventions was the wheel, and it has continued to be useful. Since then, life has become easier for many people as a result of new ideas. Most important inventions came at first from China, and later from the Middle East, Europe, and the US. There are recent signs that this is changing, and new ideas are coming from many more parts of the world. One thing, though, will never change—the ability of human beings to look at something old and think of something new.

ACTIVITIES

Chapters 1–3

Before you read

1 What do you think is the greatest invention that has ever been made? Why? Discuss your choice with other students.

2 Look at the Word List at the back of this book. Find two things that:
   a use gunpowder
   b are inside a computer
   c travel in space
   d help people navigate

3 Can you name these people?
   a the painter of the *Mona Lisa*
   b a Greek who studied triangles
   c an early Venetian traveler to China
   Discuss what you know about them with other students, or find information about them on the Internet.

While you read

4 Are these sentences true (T) or false (F)?
   a Bi Sheng printed the first Chinese book.   .....
   b Johannes Gutenberg printed the first European book.   .....
   c Euclid started a method of thinking which we still use.   .....
   d Roman numbers caused the Romans great problems.   .....
   e Before Columbus, everybody thought the world was flat.   .....
   f The time in New York is earlier than it is in London.   .....

After you read

5 You are standing in the northwest corner of a city square. Each side of the square is 100 meters long. You decide to walk straight across the square to the southeast corner. To the nearest meter, how far do you walk?

6 Discuss which of these three subjects—printing, mathematics, or navigation—has been most useful to people over the centuries. Give reasons for your opinion.

Chapters 4–6

Before you read

7 In which century do you think each of these was invented, or first happened?

   a the rifle
   b the machine gun
   c the gasoline engine
   d the high-pressure steam engine
   e the first balloon flight
   f the first powered, controlled airplane flight

8 Discuss recent changes that you know about to guns, engines, and/or flight.

While you read

9 Who:

   a defended the city of Kaifeng?   . . . .
   b invented a repeating handgun?   . . . .
   c built the first high-pressure steam engine
      in America?   . . . .
   d invented the jet engine?   . . . .
   e flew from a tall building in Istanbul?   . . . .
   f first flew an airplane from France to England? . . . .

After you read

10 Match each person on the left with a person on the right. What are these pairs of people known for?

a Hezarfen Celebi	Hiram Maxim
b Jacques Charles	Charles Lindbergh
c Gottlieb Daimler	Abbas Ibn Firnas
d Amelia Earhart	Richard Trevithick
e Oliver Evans	Nikolaus Otto
f Richard Gatling	Joseph Montgolfier

11 James Watt invented new steam engines, but for twenty-five years he stopped anyone else from making them. During this time, he grew rich. Do you think Watt was right? Discuss this with another student.

Chapters 7–9

Before you read

12 Write a list of all the ways that a person could, in the past, and can, at present, send a message to someone in another part of the country. Compare your list with another student's. Which of you has the longest list?

13 Discuss these two inventions: television and the Internet. How have they changed people's lives? What good have they done? What harm do they do?

While you read

14 Match each person with the correct country. Draw lines between them.

a	Claude Chappe	France
b	Samuel Morse	Russia
c	Paul Julius Reuter	Scotland
d	Guglielmo Marconi	Italy
e	John Logie Baird	Switzerland
f	Vladimir Kosmo Zworykin	US
g	George de Mestral	Germany

After you read

15 Choose a photograph from chapters 7–9. Describe what you can see in the picture. Why was this invention important? What came before or after it?

16 Write notes for a speech about something that was invented in your country. What was it? When was it invented? Who was the inventor? How did it change people's lives? Did it change the inventor's life? Give your speech and then answer questions from other students.

Writing

17 Imagine that you are living in Pythagoras's school in Crotone, in the sixth century B.C. You eat only vegetables and spend your time learning about mathematics and music. Write a letter to a friend describing life in the school, and whether you like it or not.

18 Alexander Graham Bell always refused to have a telephone in his house. Write a letter from Bell to a friend explaining how the telephone can help people, but why he doesn't want one himself.

19 In the 1930s, a company lawyer had to tell a US court why he thought that Philo Farnsworth was the real inventor of television. Find out more about Farnsworth's work, from books or the Internet, and write a speech for the lawyer.

20 Imagine that you are Trevor Bayliss, in 1994. You have appeared on *Tomorrow's World*, and now a newspaper wants you to write about why you built the new radio and how it can help people. Write 200 words.

21 Imagine the world 100 years from now. Will life be better for most people, or will new ways of making war mean that Earth is a more dangerous place? Write about your ideas.

22 Choose the inventor in this book that you are most interested in. Use information from this and other books, and from the Internet, and write the story of their life.

Answers for the activities in this book are available from the Penguin Readers website:
www.penguinreaders.com
A free Factsheet for this book is also available from this website.